Who has a trumpet nose?

Contents

Who is a mammal?

You are! Mammals are living things which are different from other living things in specific ways. For example, they are warm-blooded and most have hair. You have lots of tiny hairs all over your body. Other mammals, such as dogs and rabbits, have hair that is much longer and thicker. This is called fur. And almost all mammals give birth to live young instead of laying eggs.

Who drinks milk?

All baby mammals drink milk when they are young. They drink milk from their mother. This is called suckling. When they are older, they eat solid food.

What does fur do?

Fur has many jobs. Polar bear fur is thick, which helps keep the bears warm in the cold places where they live. Some individual hairs in a porcupine's coat grow together to make protective quills, also called spines. The fur on baby deer, called fawns, has spots, which helps the fawns hide from enemies.

Fun Facts

The biggest mammal is the blue whale. It grows to 100 feet (30 meters) long and 150 tons in weight. That's as heavy as five giant trucks. The smallest mammal is the hog-nosed bat. Its body is as big as your thumb, and its wings are as long as your fingers.

Who has a special pocket?

Mammals called marsupials. They have something on their tummy that looks like a pocket. It is called a pouch. When the baby is born, it crawls along its mother's fur into the pouch. The baby stays in the pouch, where it drinks its mother's milk and grows bigger. Kangaroos, koalas, opossums, and quolls are all marsupials.

kangaroo

A baby kangaroo is called a joey.

Which mammal is a devil?

The Tasmanian devil, which lives on the island of Tasmania. It is also a marsupial. When devils see one another, they open their mouths wide and growl and yell at each other.

Is it a bird? Is it a plane?

It's a sugar glider. It has a flap of skin along the sides of its body that it can stretch out like wings to glide from tree to tree. These small Australian marsupials like to eat such sweet foods as sap and the gum made by trees called wattles.

quoll

Which marsupials ride piggyback?

Baby quolls! Their mother often changes their home, which is called a den. Quolls have lots of babies at a time, up to 8. The mother carries her babies to a new den on piggyback.

Who likes licking ants?

The giant anteater, which lives in the grasslands and forests of South America. When it finds an ant nest or termite mound, the anteater breaks it open with its strong front legs and huge claws. Then it uses its sticky tongue to lick up hundreds of ants or termites at one time. Its tongue is as long as your arm, so it can reach deep inside an ant nest or termite mound.

Which mammal has armor?

The armadillo. Its back is covered in hard, flat pieces called plates. The plates work like a suit of armor, to protect the armadillo from enemies. When it's threatened, the armadillo rolls into a ball with only the tough plates showing.

8

Who is a slow mover?

The sloth, which lives in the South American rain forests. The sloth hangs upside down from trees, holding on with its front and back legs. It does everything slowly and moves only one arm or leg at a time. It moves so slowly that algae—tiny living things—grow on its fur.

NOW YOU KNOW!

South America is home to armadillos, anteaters, and sloths. Some types, or species, of armadillo live farther north, in southern North America and Central America, but most species are found on the southern continent.

Fun Facts

Some mammals have no teeth at all. The giant anteater and other anteaters have no teeth. The anteater licks up ants with its long tongue and swallows them whole. It eats only termites and ants.

Who has a trumpet nose?

Elephants blow through their trunks making a noise like the sound of a trumpet! The elephant's trunk actually is a long nose and an upper lip. An elephant uses its trunk to pull leaves from trees and to pull up grass to eat. The trunk is also used for drinking and squirting water.

NOW YOU KNOW!

The three largest land animals on Earth live in Africa. African elephants are the largest, rhinoceroses are the second-largest, and hippos are third-largest. All three are mammals.

Who has a hairy nose?

A rhinoceros, whose horn is made not of bone but of a material that is like a mixture of hair and fingernails. The

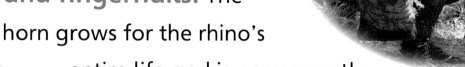

horn grows for the rhino's entire life and is permanently joined to its nose. Rhinos can push down small trees with their horns.

Fun Facts

The elephant's tusks are two long top teeth. They are very strong, and an elephant can lift as much as 2,000 pounds (900 kilograms).

Whose name means "river horse"?

The hippopotamus! Its name comes from two Greek words that mean "river horse," even though it's more closely related to whales. Hippos spend most of their time in rivers. They roam on land only at night, looking for a dinner of fruits and vegetables along the riverbank.

Who clashes antlers?

Male deer do, when they are fighting over territory. Antlers are made of bone. Usually only male deer have them. A male deer, called a buck or a stag, grows a new set of antlers every year. Each spring, new antlers start to grow. The antlers reach full size by summer. In winter, they fall off; a new set grows again in spring.

Who has a winter coat?

Bison, which live on the plains in North America. Bison, sometimes called buffalo, grow a long, brown, shaggy coat in the winter to keep warm. When the weather gets warmer, the coat gradually becomes thinner.

Are wildebeests really wild beasts?

They can be if they're attacked. Wildebeests are a kind of antelope. They can run very fast if a predator, such as a lion or hyena, threatens them. (A predator is an animal that eats other animals.) If a wildebeest has to fight, it will kick with its sharp hooves or jab with its pointed horns.

NOW YOU KNOW!

Peaceful animals face threats and have developed ways to protect themselves. Some threats come from where the animals live, as with fierce North American winters. Thick coats protect bison from the cold. Sharp body parts, like antlers, horns, and hooves, and behaviors like pronking help animals protect themselves from enemies.

Who pronks?

Antelope. Some antelope do a sort of jump known as pronking, perhaps to show enemies that they're healthy and will be hard to catch. They leap straight up into the air with their legs stiff, as if they're bouncing on a trampoline!

Who carries a grocery store?

The camel, in its hump.
Camels live in the desert and often have to go for a long time without anything to eat. So the camel builds up a store of food in its hump. The hump is made of fat, which the camel uses when it needs energy.

Do zebras wear pajamas?

No, but their striped hides look like pajamas. Zebras live in Africa and eat grass. Each zebra has a slightly different pattern of stripes on its hide. The patterns may help zebras recognize one another.

Who needs water?

All animals, even camels. But camels can last for weeks in the hot desert without drinking. They don't sweat very much, and they get some water from the plants they eat.

Where do pigs come from?

Wild pigs, boars, and hogs come from Africa, Europe, and Asia. Explorers and colonists brought hogs to North and South America in the 1500s.

Who has teeth growing out of its nose?

The babirusa, a wild pig from Indonesia. A male babirusa has tusks in its upper jaw. A tusk is a long tooth. The babirusa's tusks grow up instead of down. They poke up through the skin of its nose. Sometimes the tusks grow long enough to touch the babirusa's forehead.

Who makes a pond?

Beavers, when they build dams.
They cut down trees using their four hard, sharp front teeth and pull the trees across a stream to make a dam. Water builds up behind the dam to form a pond. The beavers cut down more twigs and branches to build a large, domed nest in the pond. This nest is called a lodge.

Fun Facts

There is a gap between a beaver's front, wood-gnawing teeth and the back, chewing teeth. Skin slides through the gap and keeps splinters from getting into the beaver's throat when it's cutting down a tree.

Which mammal is your secret housemate?

The house mouse. It is so tiny you may not know when one is living in your house. The mouse will nibble your food and eat any crumbs you drop on the floor. It will make a nest somewhere cozy, such as under the floorboards. A brown rat may also come into the house. A rat is bigger than a mouse.

NOW YOU KNOW!

Beavers, mice, rats, and squirrels are all rodents. They have front teeth, called incisors, that grow their entire lives. These incisors are specially made for gnawing hard things like trees and acorns. The gnawing wears down the teeth so they can't grow too long.

How do squirrels plant trees?

They bury nuts in the ground. In the fall, squirrels feast on acorns, chestnuts, and other seeds. If there are too many to eat at once, the squirrel buries them for later. Some of these seeds grow into new trees.

Who hangs around?

Bats, because they can't stand up on their legs. Bats live all around the world except where it's very cold. They rest and sleep hanging upside down from trees and in caves. Bats sleep during the day and fly around at night looking for food. Most bats eat insects, fruit, and such small animals as frogs.

Who has sharp hairs?

The hedgehog's spines are long, thick, and sharply pointed. When the hedgehog is in danger, it curls into a prickly ball to protect its face, legs, and underside. Hedgehogs snuffle around at night, feeding on insects, snakes, and bird eggs.

Are there moon rats on the moon?

No, but there are moon rats in Asian forests. These insect-eating mammals are like hedgehogs, but they have fur instead of spines and a long, scaly tail like a rat. The largest kind of moon rat is the size of a rabbit.

NOW YOU KNOW!

Animals that eat bugs are called insectivores.

Which mammal never sees sun?

The mole, who lives almost all of its life underground. It has strong front paws with huge

claws to help it dig tunnels. It eats worms, grubs, and other small animals it finds in the ground.

Who howls at night?

Wolves howl to one another at night. Wolves live together in groups called packs and howl to tell other members in the pack where they are. Wolves eat such large herbivores (animals that eat plants) as deer, bison, and caribou. They also howl to warn wolves in other packs to stay away.

Fun Facts

Wolves don't just howl. They make lots of other noises, such as yipping, barking, growling, and whining.

How many names does a mountain lion have?

Four! The mountain lion is also called a cougar, panther, or puma, depending on where it lives. Mountain lions live in deserts, mountains, and forests, and near ranches, where they occasionally attack farm animals.

NOW YOU KNOW!

Animals that eat meat are called carnivores. All the larger mammals you see here—the wolves, tigers, and mountain lions—are carnivores.

Do tigers like water?

Yes! A tiger in the jungles of Asia keeps cool by lazing in a river or swampy pool. It hunts at night when it's cooler.

A tiger hunts many kinds of large animals, such as wild pigs, deer, and antelope.

Which bears fish?

Brown bears enjoy fishing. They sit at the top of a waterfall, and as the fish leap over the waterfall, the bears catch them in their claws or mouth. Some brown bears are called grizzly bears because their fur is grizzled. This means some white hairs grow in with the brown, making the fur seem streaked with gray.

Who loves to eat bamboo?

The giant panda. Pandas live in bamboo forests in the mountains of China. Bamboo is the main food that a panda eats. It spends more than 12 hours a day eating bamboo stalks and leaves.

Who wears a mask?

Raccoons, who live in North America. They are nocturnal, which means they sleep all day and hunt for food at night. They often live near people and raid garbage cans for food. Markings around their eyes look just like a mask.

Fun Facts

A Kodiak bear is the largest land carnivore. It is a type of grizzly bear that lives only on Kodiak Island, near Alaska. It can weigh nearly 1,200 pounds (780 kilograms).

Where would you find cubs in a holt?

Along a riverbank. A holt is the name of the burrow, a space in the ground, where a mother otter raises her family. Otter babies are called cubs or pups. They splash about in the water learning to catch food, such as fish and frogs.

Is an elephant seal big?

An adult male elephant seal is huge and can weigh the same as a female elephant—nearly 8,800 pounds (4,000 kilograms). These mammals are called elephant seals because the males have a nose like a short trunk. When they are ready to mate, elephant seals throw back their heads and make loud roaring noises. Elephant seals move very slowly on land but are good swimmers and divers. They spend most of their time in the water.

Do crabeater seals eat crabs?

No! They live on floating pieces of ice called ice floes in the ocean around Antarctica, where there are no crabs at all. These seals eat small, shrimp-like animals called krill. They rest and breed on the ice and feed in the water.

crabeater seals

Do elephant seals have tusks?

No, the walrus has long, strong tusks. It uses them to impress females and as weapons to fight off enemies. It also uses its tusks to pull itself out of the water onto the ice.

Is that a seal or a cow?

manatee

Sometimes called sea cows, manatees and dugongs look like big seals, but they do **not eat fish.** They are slow, peaceful plant-eaters.

Which mammal sings?

Great whales, such as the humpback, "sing" to each other. Each year the songs of humpback whales change slightly. Scientists think male humpbacks sing to warn off other male humpbacks. Both male and female whales make such noises as hums, whistles, wails, groans, and grunts.

Do dolphins do somersaults?

Yes! Dolphins at sea sometimes jump out of the water and spin around. No one knows why they do this. It's possible this is a way of talking to one another, or they might do it just because it's fun!

Which mammal eats with a comb?

The blue whale. In oceans all over the world, the blue whale feeds on krill and other tiny sea animals. It filters these from the seawater using stiff plates in its mouth called baleen, which work like a huge comb or sieve. Blue whales are the largest animal that ever lived—larger than any dinosaur!

Fun Facts

Beluga whales are known as sea canaries. They produce an astonishing array of whistles, clicks, and shrieks.

How low can you go?

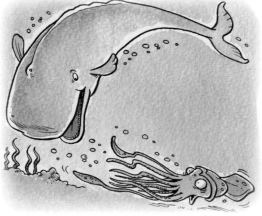

3,300 feet (1,000 meters)! The sperm whale is able to hold its breath for more than one hour at a time when it dives deep into the ocean to catch large squid, its main food.

Who has a handy tail?

The spider monkey, which lives in the Amazon rain forests of South America. It can hang by its tail and grab food with its hands and feet. Or it can hang by one hand and grab food with its feet and its tail! A tail like this, which can be used like an extra hand, is called a prehensile tail.

Fun Facts

A very large animal nose belongs to the male proboscis monkey. The long, floppy nose droops right over his mouth and down to his chin.

proboscis monkey

Which monkey is the smallest?

The pygmy marmoset. This tiny monkey is the size of your hand. It eats fruits and grubs and drinks the sap from trees.

Who makes the most noise?

The howler monkey of South America is one of the loudest of all animals. Its deafening shouts and whoops can be heard as far as 2 miles (3.2 kilometers) away. It howls to let other howlers know where it is, and also when it meets another group of howlers.

howler monkey

spider monkey

What do you call a baboon group?

A troop! Baboons are big monkeys that live in Africa and on the southwestern part of the Arabian Peninsula. As many as 200 baboons live in one troop. A baby stays with its mother until it's about 18 months old.

baboon

Do mammals use tools?

Yes, to help do things they can't do with bare hands (or paws). Human beings are expert tool users, but chimpanzees are a clever second. In Africa, chimps use rocks to crack open nuts or to split bones. Some chimps use a leaf as a cup to scoop up water. Chimps also use twigs as a tool to reach food. They'll poke twigs into termite nests. The termites in the nest cling to the twigs. The chimps pull out the twigs and eat the termites.

Which mammals learned sign language?

A gorilla. Scientists in California taught several hundred signs to a female gorilla named Koko. (Sign languages use movements of the hands, body, and face instead of spoken sounds to make messages.) Gorillas, which live in the rain forests of equatorial Africa, are one of the world's most intelligent animals.

Fun Facts

Great apes like chimps aren't the only mammals that use tools. Sea otters pound clams against a rock balanced on their chest to get at the tasty meat inside.

Why do apes sing songs every day?

No one knows exactly why female and male gibbons sing a duet known as the "great call." Some scientists think the duet is a way the gibbons tell other animals what land belongs to the gibbons. Gibbons have arms that are longer and stronger than their legs. They swing hand-over-hand in the forests of Southeast Asia.

Index

© 2013 Southwestern Advantage
Reprinted in 2014
Nashville, Tennessee
ISBN 978-0-87197-581-2
www.southwesternadvantage.com

Originally published as *Ask Me*
Southwestern/Great American, Inc.
© 2002, 2005, 2010, 2011, 2012
Southwestern Advantage
Nashville, Tennessee
ISBN 0-87197-518-1

Printed by RR Donnelley, China

Henry Bedford
Chief Executive Officer, Southwestern/ Great American, Inc.

Dan Moore
President, Southwestern Advantage

Curriculum Director
Janet D. Sweet

Art Director
Travis Rader

Production Manager
Powell Ropp

The publisher would like to thank the following editors and designers who contributed to the original work in this book: Mary Cummings, Judy Jackson, Barbara J. Reed, Steve Newman, Starletta Polster, Sara Anglin, Jessie Anglin

The publishers would like to thank the following artists whose work appears in this book: Barbara Ball, John Butler, Steve Caldwell, Jim Channell, Kuo Kang Chen, Andrew Clark, Mark Davis, Peter Dennis, Heather Dickinson, Richard Draper, James Field, Nicholas Forder, Chris Forsey, Mike Foster/Maltings Partnership, Terry Gabbey, Alan Hancocks, Richard Hook, John James, Emma Jones, Tony Kenyon, Aziz Khan, Sue King/SGA, Kevin Maddison, Janos Marffy, Debbie Meekcoms, Helen Parsley, Rachel Philips, Jane Pickering, Neil Reid, Terry Riley, Pete Roberts, Steve Roberts, Martin Sanders, Peter Sarson, Mike Saunders, Sarah Smith, Studio Galante, Rudi Vizi, Mike White, Peter Wilks, Paul Williams.

Images/art © Thinkstock:
People and Places: pages 15, 17
Planet Earth: page 5